Baseball Quizzes

JOHN GRAFTON

DOVER PUBLICATIONS, INC.
New York

Copyright

Copyright © 1994 by Dover Publications, Inc.
All rights reserved under Pan American and International Copyright Conventions.

Published in Canada by General Publishing Company, Ltd., 30 Lesmill Road, Don Mills, Toronto, Ontario.
Published in the United Kingdom by Constable and Company, Ltd., 3 The Lanchesters, 162–164 Fulham Palace Road, London W6 9ER.

Bibliographical Note

Baseball Quizzes is a new work, first published by Dover Publications, Inc., in 1994.

Library of Congress Cataloging-in-Publication Data

Grafton, John.
    Baseball quizzes / John Grafton.
        p.   cm.
    ISBN 0-486-27855-7
    1. Baseball—United States—Miscellanea.
GV867.3.G73   1994
796.357′0973—dc20
                                                                94–33503
                                                                CIP

Manufactured in the United States of America
Dover Publications, Inc., 31 East 2nd Street, Mineola, N.Y. 11501

Introduction

WHO CAN BOAST more career hits, Willie Mays or Carl
Yastrzemski? Who did the Yankees trade to the San Francisco
Giants for Bobby Bonds on October 22, 1974? Who was victorious
in the 1920 World Series? And what major leaguer was known by
the sobriquet "Pie"?

These and many other posers, in a variety of categories, await
you herein. There is no such thing as trivia where the ritual and
romance of baseball is concerned, and in this book you will
encounter topics ranging from the big wins to the most unusual
nicknames. These quizzes, a challenge for old-timers and a train-
ing ground for rookies, will improve the mettle of any baseball
fan. Whatever your level of engagement with our national pas-
time, you will come away privy to baseball lore that will stand you
in good stead at any gathering of die-hards. And finally, of course,
it is a good read.

If you are stumped, the answer to each question is in the back
of the book.

Contents

A True–False Baseball History Quiz

1. The Cleveland Indians won more games in a single season than any other American League team.

2. Warren Spahn was the first pitcher to win back-to-back Cy Young awards.

3. Next to Cy Young's 511, Christy Mathewson won the most games as a pitcher.

4. Tom Seaver won more games in his career than either Lefty Grove or Early Wynn.

5. In 1969, the first year for divisional play, the Mets got to the Series by beating Atlanta while Baltimore got in by beating Oakland.

6. Babe Ruth was the only Yankee to lead the AL in home runs during the 1920s.

7. Roy Sievers was the last Washington Senator to lead the AL in home runs.

8. Dale Murphy was the last National Leaguer to lead the league in home runs three straight years.

9. Ryne Sandberg, with 40 in 1990, is the only Chicago Cub player to lead the NL in home runs since Ernie Banks did it in 1960.

10. San Francisco's Willie Mays was the first player on a West Coast team to lead the NL in home runs.

11. Oakland's Reggie Jackson was the first player on a West Coast team to lead the AL in home runs.

12. Willie Mays was the first player on a West Coast team in either league to lead the league in home runs in two consecutive years.

13. Ted Williams was the last Red Sox player to lead the AL in runs batted in for two consecutive years.

14. Mickey Mantle was the last Yankee player to lead the AL in runs batted in for two consecutive years.

15. No National Leaguer has driven in more than 150 runs in a season since Tommy Davis of the Dodgers drove in 153 in 1962.

16. No American Leaguer has driven in more than 140 runs in a season since Washington's Harmon Killebrew drove in exactly 140 in 1969.

17. Lou Gehrig's 184 RBIs for the 1931 Yankees is the all-time single season RBI record.

18. The .370 league-leading batting average compiled by San Diego's Tony Gwynn in 1987 is the highest in the NL since World War II.

19. Tony Gwynn's .313 in 1988 is the lowest league-leading batting average in the NL since World War II.

20. Tony Gwynn's .313 average in 1988 is the lowest ever to lead the NL.

21. Elmer Flick of Cleveland had the lowest-ever league-leading batting average in the AL—.308 in 1905.

22. Since Ted Williams batted .406 in 1941, Wade Boggs had the highest single-season average in the AL.

23. The last National Leaguer to bat .400 was Stan Musial.

24. Between Mickey Mantle in 1956 and Don Mattingly in 1984, no Yankee led the AL in batting.

25. Hank Aaron hit the most home runs ever, but never led the NL in batting average for a season.

26. George Sisler had the highest single-season batting average of any player in the 1920s.

27. Roberto Clemente had the highest single-season batting average of any NL player in the 1960s.

28. And Clemente's best single season average in the 1960s was higher than any AL player in the decade as well.

29. Rickey Henderson was the first player on a California team to lead the AL in batting average for a season.

30. Since 1970, no ballplayer has won batting titles more than ten years apart.

31. Since Philadelphia's Steve Carlton led the NL with a 1.98 earned-run average in 1972, when he pitched 346 innings, no other NL ERA leader has pitched over 300 innings in his league-leading season.

32. In the same time period, no AL ERA leader pitched more innings in his league-leading year than Carlton's 346.

33. Between Ron Guidry in 1978 and 1979 and Roger Clemens in 1990 and 1991, no pitcher in either league won back-to-back ERA titles.

34. Wrigley Field in Chicago has the smallest seating capacity of any current major league ballpark.

35. There has never been a tie vote for a Most Valuable Player award.

36. Tommy Davis was the first player on a California team to be the NL's MVP.

37. Oakland's Vida Blue was the first player on a California team to be the AL's MVP.

38. Frank Howard was the only Washington Senator ever named AL MVP.

39. Stan Musial was the first National Leaguer to win two MVP awards.

40. Stan Musial was the first National Leaguer to win three MVP awards.

41. Jimmie Foxx was the first American Leaguer to win two MVP awards.

42. Between Mickey Mantle in 1962 and Don Mattingly in 1985 only one Yankee was the AL's MVP.

43. Three members of Cincinnati's "Big Red Machine" were NL MVP winners.

44. The last American Leaguer to win back-to-back MVP awards was Roger Maris.

45. Two New York Met pitchers have been the NL Rookie of the Year.

46. Between 1955 and 1990, Fred Lynn was the only Red Sox outfielder to be the AL's Rookie of the Year.

47. No team has ever had more than three consecutive Rookies of the Year.

48. There are four Hall of Fame members with the same last name.

49. The first All-Star Game was played at Yankee Stadium in New York.

50. Between Catfish Hunter's 4–0 perfect game for Oakland against Minnesota in 1968 and Mike Witt's 1–0 perfect game for California against Texas in 1984 there were no major league perfect games.

51. The two teams other than the Yankees that won AL pennants in the 1950s were both managed by the same man.

52. John McGraw was the first manager in the twentieth century to win three consecutive pennants.

53. Baltimore's Earl Weaver was the first manager in either league to win three consecutive pennants after the start of divisional play in 1969.

54. Tommy Lasorda was the first NL manager to win two consecutive pennants after the start of divisional play in 1969.

55. Since 1960, Dick Allen is the only Chicago White Sox player to lead the AL in home runs.

56. Mickey Mantle was the only AL player to lead the league in home runs two or more times during the 1950s.

57. Duke Snider was the only Dodger player to lead the NL in home runs during the 1950s.

58. The Los Angeles Dodgers didn't have a single NL home run leader in the 1970s or the 1980s.

59. Duke Snider was the only Dodger player to lead the NL in runs batted in for a season during the 1950s.

60. Willie Mays was the single Giant player to lead the NL in runs batted in for a season during the 1950s.

61. Detroit's Cecil Fielder is the first AL player to lead the league in RBIs three consecutive years since Babe Ruth did this in 1919–1921.

62. Joe Medwick was the last National League player to lead the league in RBIs in three consecutive seasons.

63. Mike Schmidt was the only Philadelphia player to lead the NL in RBIs during the 1980s.

64. Jim Rice, who shared the 1983 AL RBI lead with Milwaukee's Cecil Cooper, was the only Red Sox player to lead the league in RBIs in the 1980s.

65. George Bell was the first Toronto player to lead the AL in batting for a season.

66. No West Coast player has won an AL batting title since 1980.

67. No New York Met player has ever won an NL batting title.

68. No Dodger player has won the NL batting title since Tommy Davis in 1963.

69. No Minnesota Twin other than Tony Oliva and Rod Carew ever won an AL batting title.

70. Tony Gwynn is the only San Diego player ever to win an NL batting title.

71. Colorado's Andres Galarraga, who led the NL with a .370 batting average in 1993, is the only player to win a batting title in a team's first year in existence.

72. No player on a team based in Texas has ever won a batting title in either league.

73. Roger Clemens is the only Red Sox pitcher to win the Cy Young award.

74. Sparky Lyle is the last Yankee to win the Cy Young.

75. Fernando Valenzuela in 1981 was the first Dodger since Sandy Koufax to win the Cy Young.

76. Tom Glavine, the 1991 NL Cy Young winner, was the first Braves pitcher to win the award since Warren Spahn in 1957.

77. No pitcher on a Texas-based team has ever won the Cy Young in either league.

78. Bret Saberhagen is the only Royals pitcher to win the Cy Young.

79. Vernon Law, the 1960 Cy Young winner, is the only Pittsburgh pitcher to win the award.

80. Yankee Bob Grim in 1954 was the first pitcher in either league to win the Rookie of the Year award.

81. Boston's Walt Dropo in 1950 was the first first baseman in either league to win the Rookie of the Year award.

82. Outfielder Bob Allison was the only Washington Senator ever to win the Rookie of the Year award.

83. In 1990 Cleveland's Sandy Alomar, Jr. was the first catcher to win the AL Rookie of the Year award since Carleton Fisk in 1972.

84. In 1987 San Diego's Benito Santiago was the first catcher to win the NL Rookie of the Year award since Johnny Bench in 1968.

85. The last Philadelphia Phillie to win the Rookie of the Year award was Dick Allen in 1964.

86. Pete Rose, the 1963 NL Rookie of the Year, was the first Red to win the award.

87. In 1967 New York Met Tom Seaver was the first Rookie of the Year to play on an expansion team.

88. Jackie Robinson, Sandy Koufax, Mickey Mantle, Willie Mays and Tom Seaver are the only players who ever played on New York teams to be elected to the Hall of Fame during their first year of eligibility.

89. Johnny Bench is the only catcher elected to the Hall of Fame in his first year of eligibility.

90. Outfielder Al Kaline is the only Detroit Tiger elected to the Hall of Fame in his first year of eligibility.

91. Nolan Ryan pitched more of his seven no-hitters for Texas than for any of his other teams.

92. Pete Rose is the only player with more than 14,000 times at bat in the major leagues.

93. Philadelphia's Veterans Stadium has the largest seating capacity of any current National League ballpark.

94. Fenway Park is the only current major league ballpark with a home run distance to center field less than 400 feet.

95. Met Dwight Gooden was the only pitcher on a New York team to lead his league in ERA during the 1980s.

96. Boston's Roger Clemens is the only AL pitcher since 1980 to lead the league in ERA with a mark under 2.00.

97. Of the top ten all-time home run leaders, only Babe Ruth and Jimmie Foxx were active in the major leagues before World War II.

98. Of the ten pitchers with the most lifetime shutouts, only

Warren Spahn, Tom Seaver and Nolan Ryan were active after World War II.

99. Pete Rose got the most hits, but Ty Cobb scored more runs.

100. Carl Yastrzemski got more hits in his career than Willie Mays.

World Series History

1. Since World War II, has there been a four-game sweep in the World Series that did not involve a New York team?

2. The Yankees hold the record for appearing in 33 World Series. What team has played in the Series next most often?

3. Only one player in baseball history has played on the winning team in the World Series ten times. Who was that?

4. Who are the two players tied for the most career stolen bases in the World Series?

5. When was the first World Series night game?

6. When and where did the largest crowd attend a World Series game?

7. Is the player who holds the record for most hits in a World Series game a member of a New York team?

8. As one might expect, Babe Ruth is one of the two players who hit three home runs in a World Series game. Who is the other one? Did either one do this more than once?

9. Can you name the three National Leaguers who share the record (three) for stolen bases in a World Series game?

10. Can you name the American Leaguer who is the only player ever to get four hits in two games of the same Series?

11. What pitcher recorded the most strikeouts in a World Series game?

12. Who drove in the most runs in a single World Series game?

13. Since World War II, only three players have stolen home in a World Series game. How many can you name?

14. Who had the highest batting average for a single World Series?

15. Who hit the most home runs in a single World Series?

16. What pitcher recorded the most strikeouts in a four-game Series?

17. What pitcher recorded the most strikeouts in a Series of any length?

18. The Yankees hold the record with five players who hit a home run in their first time at bat in the World Series. How many of them can you name?

19. What's the record for most career wins in the World Series by a pitcher who never lost a World Series game?

20. Who was the oldest pitcher to pitch a complete World Series game?

Miscellaneous Multiple Choice

1. Who was the youngest player to appear in a World Series game?

Phil Rizzuto
Freddie Lindstrom
Dizzy Dean
Grover Cleveland Alexander

2. Who was the oldest player to appear in a World Series game?

Mickey Mantle
Bob Gibson
Jack Quinn
Leo Durocher

3. Who was the youngest player-manager to manage a team for a complete season?

John McGraw
Lou Boudreau
Ty Cobb
Rogers Hornsby

4. Who was the youngest player to win the American League batting title?

Carl Yastrzemski
Al Kaline
Jackie Jensen
Goose Goslin

5. Who was the youngest player to win the National League batting title?

Willie Mays
Joe Morgan
Pete Reiser
Mel Ott

6. Who was the oldest player to win the American League batting title?

Mickey Cochrane
Ted Williams
Harry Heilmann
Norm Cash

7. Who was the oldest player to win the National League batting title?

Bill Terry
Carl Furillo
Honus Wagner
Rogers Hornsby

8. Who was the youngest American League Cy Young award winner?

Bret Saberhagen
Ron Guidry
Whitey Ford
Mike Garcia

9. Who was the youngest National League Cy Young award winner?

Bob Gibson
Juan Marichal
Dwight Gooden
Orel Hershiser

10. Who was the oldest American League Cy Young award winner?

Don Larsen
Tommy John
Early Wynn
Luis Tiant

11. Who was the oldest National League Cy Young award winner?

Robin Roberts
Steve Carlton
Nolan Ryan
Don Newcombe

12. The first catcher to be named American League MVP was:

Yogi Berra
Bill Dickey
Mickey Cochrane
Luke Sewell

13. The first 1st baseman to win the National League MVP award was:

Bill Terry
Phil Cavaretta
Frank McCormick
Dolf Camilli

14. Since the World Series MVP award was instituted in 1955, the first non-pitcher to win it was:

Mickey Mantle
Duke Snider
Bobby Richardson
Frank Robinson

15. The first player on a West Coast team to win it was:

Larry Sherry
Sandy Koufax
Willie Mays
Tommy Davis

16. The first catcher to win the American League Rookie of the
    Year award was:

Carlton Fisk
Thurman Munson
Elston Howard
Sherm Lollar

17. The Gold Glove award was inaugurated in 1957. What Ameri-
    can League pitcher won it the first four years?

Whitey Ford
Bobby Shantz
Frank Lary
Jim Kaat

18. The last American League pitcher to win the Gold Glove five
    consecutive years was:

Ron Guidry
Jim Kaat
Mark Langston
Jim Palmer

19. The National League pitcher to win the Gold Glove the most
    consecutive years was:

Steve Carlton
Phil Niekro
Bob Gibson
Tom Seaver

20. The first National Leaguer to pitch a perfect game after Sandy Koufax in 1965 was:

Dock Ellis
Tom Browning
Tom Seaver
Nolan Ryan

21. The first American Leaguer to pitch a perfect game after Don Larsen in 1956 was:

Jim Bunning
Jim Palmer
Catfish Hunter
Joel Horlen

22. Who was the last American League pitcher before Don Larsen's 1956 game to pitch a perfect game?

Allie Reynolds
Charlie Robertson
Wes Ferrell
Howard Ehmke

23. Before Koufax' 1965 perfect game, the last National Leaguer to pitch a perfect game was:

Jim Maloney
Lew Burdette
Warren Spahn
Jim Bunning

24. The first twentieth-century perfect game in either league was pitched by:

Cy Young
Walter Johnson
Deacon Philippe
Dazzy Vance

25. The player with the highest slugging average for a single season is:

Ted Williams
Babe Ruth
Lou Gehrig
Mickey Mantle

26. The player who got the most hits in a single season is:

Babe Ruth
Pete Rose
Ted Williams
George Sisler

27. Who is the National Leaguer with the most home runs in a single season?

Willie Mays
Hack Wilson
Hank Aaron
Ralph Kiner

28. Since 1920 the player with the most triples in a season is:

Rod Carew
Rogers Hornsby
Kiki Cuyler
Mel Ott

29. The player with the record for most times at bat in a single season is:

Pete Rose
Joe Morgan
Willie Wilson
Omar Moreno

30. Who is the player with the most doubles in a single season since World War II?

Willie Mays
George Kell
Hal McRae
Don Mattingly

31. The player who received the most bases on balls in a single season is:

Ted Williams
Mickey Mantle
Babe Ruth
Lou Gehrig

32. Which player struck out the most times in a single season?

Babe Ruth
Bobby Bonds
Mickey Mantle
Reggie Jackson

33. The player who got the most pinch hits in a single season is:

Dave Philley
Jose Morales
Smoky Burgess
Rusty Staub

34. Only one catcher ever completed an entire season of 100 or more games with a fielding average of 1.000. He was:

Johnny Bench
Gary Carter
Buddy Rosar
Carlton Fisk

35. Only one first baseman has ever completed an entire season with a fielding average of 1.000. He was:

Lou Gehrig
Steve Garvey
Vic Power
Don Mattingly

36. What outfielder recorded the most assists in a single season in the twentieth century?

Jimmy Piersall
Richie Ashburn
Chuck Klein
Willie Mays

37. The highest career batting average for any player active since World War II is held by:

Ted Williams
Wade Boggs
George Brett
Rod Carew

38. The player who played in the most games lifetime was:

Hank Aaron
Ty Cobb
Pete Rose
Stan Musial

39. What player whose career was over before World War II played in the most games lifetime?

Babe Ruth
Eddie Collins
Ty Cobb
Honus Wagner

40. What player who played at least part of his career as a Yankee played in the most games lifetime?

Lou Gehrig
Dave Winfield
Reggie Jackson
Yogi Berra

41. Only one player hit more doubles in his career than Pete Rose did. He was:

Ty Cobb
Stan Musial
George Brett
Tris Speaker

42. Who is the only player with more than 300 career triples?

Sam Crawford
Ty Cobb
Paul Waner
Goose Goslin

43. Who holds the record for most pinch hits in a career?

Smoky Burgess
Rusty Staub
Jose Morales
Manny Mota

44. The only player to steal more than 1,000 bases in his career is:

Lou Brock
Rickey Henderson
Ty Cobb
Honus Wagner

45. Reggie Jackson is the all-time career strikeout leader with 2,597. What National Leaguer struck out the most times in his career?

Hank Aaron
Willie Stargell
Mike Schmidt
Dave Parker

46. Only one outfielder recorded more career assists than Ty Cobb. He was:

Tris Speaker
Max Carey
Richie Ashburn
Stan Musial

47. In his whole career, which player scored the most World Series runs?

Babe Ruth
Mickey Mantle
Yogi Berra
Joe DiMaggio

48. The player who got the most World Series hits in his career is:

Babe Ruth
Mickey Mantle
Yogi Berra
Joe DiMaggio

49. Only one pitcher recorded four career shutouts in World Series play. He was:

Whitey Ford
Bob Gibson
Christy Mathewson
Sandy Koufax

50. Only one pitcher recorded ten career World Series wins. Who was he?

Whitey Ford
Christy Mathewson
Lefty Gomez
Bob Gibson

Trades

A lot of baseball history revolves around the trading of players from one team to another. Here are questions about some of baseball's most important and memorable trades.

1. On December 11, 1959, the Yankees sent Hank Bauer, Don Larsen, Norm Siebern and Marv Throneberry to Kansas City in exchange for Joe DeMaestri, Kent Hadley and what other player?

2. Name the pitcher the Oakland Athletics sent to the San Francisco Giants on March 15, 1978 in return for seven players and $390,000. (If you can name more than two of the seven, you're an expert.)

3. Who did the Yankees trade to the San Francisco Giants for Bobby Bonds on October 22, 1974?

4. When the Yankees traded Bonds to the California Angels on December 11, 1975, who did they get for him?

5. The New York Mets made headlines before the 1992 season by signing free agent Bobby Bonilla to the most lucrative contract in baseball history up to that time. In 1986, who did the Chicago White Sox get for Bonilla when they traded him to Pittsburgh?

6. Name the two outstanding pitchers who figured in a trade between the Yankees and the then Boston Braves on August

23

30, 1951. Both went on to help their new teams win world championships.

7. The Phillies scored a trading grand slam on February 25, 1972 when they acquired a pitcher from the Cardinals who went on to win 20 or more games for them five times. Who was the pitcher the Phillies acquired, and who did they trade for him?

8. The Mets solidified their position as one of the top teams of the second half of the 1980s with two key trades, one in 1983 and one in 1984. Name the catcher and first baseman the Mets acquired through these trades, and the players they gave up for them.

9. When the Yankees sent first baseman Danny Cater to the Red Sox on March 22, 1972, they acquired a pitcher who figured prominently in their World Championship seasons of 1977 and 1978. Who was he?

10. What future Yankee manager did the Yankees trade to Kansas City on June 15, 1957 in exchange for what relief pitcher? Can you name at least two of the other six players involved in this deal?

11. What two teams traded their managers?

12. Going back a bit into early major league history, who did the New York Giants send to Cincinnati for future Hall of Famer Christy Mathewson in 1900? A clue: The pitcher the Giants traded away for Mathewson won belated election to the Hall of Fame himself in 1977.

13. Who did the Mets send to the Giants in 1972 for Willie Mays?

14. Name the two NL shortstops who were traded for each other in 1966.

15. Who did Oakland send to the Cubs in exchange for Ken Holtzman in 1971?

16. Who did the Orioles trade to Cincinnati after the 1965 season for Frank Robinson?

17. In what is often mentioned as a classic bad trade, who did the Mets give up for Joe Foy in 1969?

18. Not to pick on the Mets—all teams make bad trades at one time or another—but who did they give up in 1971 for Jim Fregosi?

19. Yankee fans often think about the players who got away, but the team scored well in a 1975 trade when they sent Doc Medich to the Pirates. Who did they get?

All-Star Games

1. Who were the winning and losing managers in the first All-Star Game in 1933?

2. Who is the only player to hit a grand slam home run in an All-Star Game?

3. Can you name the five players who hit two home runs in an All-Star Game?

4. Who was the oldest winning pitcher in an All-Star Game?

5. Who was the youngest player to appear in an All-Star Game?

6. Name the five great sluggers Carl Hubbell struck out consecutively in the 1934 All-Star Game in one of baseball's most memorable individual feats.

7. Who holds the record for career stolen bases in All-Star Games?

8. Can you name the three players who appeared in a record 24 All-Star Games?

9. Which of those three holds the record for most home runs in All-Star play?

10. Does one of the three hold the record for most RBIs in All-Star play?

Home Runs

1. Of the top ten home run hitters of all time, how many, in addition to Babe Ruth, Willie Mays and Mickey Mantle, played for New York teams?

2. Of all the players in major league history with 350 or more career home runs, how many were catchers?

3. Of all the players in major league history with 350 or more career home runs, how many played for the Brooklyn Dodgers?

4. Who is the last player to hit 50 or more home runs in one season?

5. Who was the last before him?

6. Who led his league in home runs the most times?

7. Who hit the most home runs in a season in his home ballpark?

8. Between Babe Ruth's 54 home runs in 1928 and Mickey Mantle's 52 home runs in 1956, two American Leaguers hit 50 or more home runs in a season. Who were they?

9. Since 1940, have any Yankees other than Joe DiMaggio, Mickey Mantle, Roger Maris and Reggie Jackson led the American League in home runs?

10. Who came to bat the most times in one season without hitting a single home run?

11. Who was the last player for the St. Louis Browns to lead the American League in home runs?

12. Who was the first African-American player to lead either league in home runs for a season?

13. Can you name the only team that had two players on it who each hit more than 50 home runs in a season?

14. Since World War II, have any players led their league in home runs in a season in which they played for more than one team?

15. Did any pitcher in the twentieth century hit three home runs in one game?

16. Did a pitcher ever hit two grand slam home runs in the same game?

17. Only once have the same two players tied each other for the league lead in home runs in more than one year, and they even did this in consecutive years. Name these two National Leaguers.

18. Duke Snider led the National League in home runs with 43 in 1956. Who was the last Brooklyn Dodger before Snider to lead the NL in home runs?

19. During the years when the Braves were in Milwaukee, did any Braves player besides Hank Aaron lead the National League in home runs?

20. Do you know what player hit the most grand slam home runs in one season?

21. Who hit the most grand slam home runs in a career?

22. Who hit the most home runs in a career without ever leading the league in that category?

23. What pitcher hit the most home runs in a career?

24. Who was the last player to hit four home runs in one game?

25. Of the other nine players who hit four home runs in one game in the twentieth century, how many can you name?

Batting Average Leaders

1. Since Ty Cobb led the American League in batting for nine straight years from 1907 through 1915, only two players have led the AL in batting as many as four consecutive years. Can you name them?

2. Who holds the National League record for leading the league in batting in the most consecutive years?

3. Did Ty Cobb have the highest batting average to win a batting title since 1900?

4. What American Leaguer holds the highest batting average for a season since World War II?

5. What National Leaguer holds the highest batting average for a season since World War II?

6. Has any player ever led the National League in batting in a year in which he played for more than one team?

7. Has any player ever led the American League in batting in a year in which he played for more than one team?

8. What player has won the most batting titles?

9. What player had the highest one season batting average which failed to win the title?

10. Six New York Yankees have led the American League in batting including Babe Ruth, Lou Gehrig, Joe DiMaggio and Mickey Mantle. Name the other two.

11. Ty Cobb led the American League in batting every year but one from 1907 through 1919. Name the player who interrupted this famous streak.

12. After Cobb's streak ended in 1919, who was the next player to lead the American League in batting for two years in a row?

13. He never led the league two years in a row, but he did lead the AL in batting in four different odd-numbered years during the 1920s. Who was he?

14. The Detroit Tigers had some great hitters in the 1960s. Name the only one who won the AL batting title.

15. Can you name the two Detroit Tigers who won the AL batting title during the 1950s?

16. And how about the one Tiger who led the AL in batting during the 1940s?

17. Did the great Brooklyn Dodger teams of the 1950s produce a National League batting champion?

18. Name the Dodger who won the NL batting title twice in a row after the team moved to Los Angeles.

19. Since 1950, how many Philadelphia Phillies have won the NL batting title?

The Great Teams and Their Players

1. The Boston team that won the first AL pennant in 1903, as well as the first World Series, had three 20-game winners. How many can you name?

2. Who led the AL in batting in that 1903 season?

3. Who lost to Boston in that first World Series?

4. What player on that team led the NL in batting in 1903?

5. The New York Giants won the NL pennants in 1904 and 1905. Who was their manager?

6. The 1904 Giants had a rare combination, two 30-game winners. Who were they?

7. The Chicago Cubs who won NL pennants in 1906, 1907 and 1908 had one of the most famous double-play combinations—shortstop, second baseman, first baseman—in history. Who were they?

8. Who played third base with this famous group?

9. Who was the manager of this Cubs team?

10. The Cubs won the Series from the Tigers in both 1907 and 1908. Name the Tiger rightfielder who led the AL in batting both of those years.

11. Who was the Hall of Famer who played center field on those great Tiger teams?

12. Who managed the AL team that won their first World Series in 1910, and then went on to win the Series in 1911 and 1913 as well?

13. Who was the righthander with a 31–9 record on that 1910 AL pennant winner? He also won three games in the 1910 World Series.

14. Who was the second baseman for the 1910 and 1911 AL pennant winners? A Hall of Famer, he was the team's top hitter both of those years.

15. Boston got back into the win column in 1912 with an AL pennant and a Series victory over the Giants. Can you name the righthander who anchored the Boston pitching staff with a 34–5 season and three wins in the Series?

16. When Boston's "Miracle Braves" won a surprise NL pennant in 1914, did they have the league's top hitter?

17. The Red Sox won back-to-back World Series in 1915 and 1916. Name the Boston outfielder who hit two home runs in the final game of the 1915 Series to defeat the Phillies.

18. Was he the first player to hit two home runs in a World Series game?

19. When the Red Sox won the 1916 Series over Brooklyn, Ernie Shore was credited with two wins, and Dutch Leonard with one. What Boston pitcher got the 4th win?

20. You're an expert if you can name the New York Giant outfielder who became the third player to hit two home runs in a World Series game with two in the 4th game in 1917.

21. Name the Hall of Famer who recorded three wins for the winning team in 1917.

22. Who hit the only home run in the "Black Sox" Series of 1919?

23. The 1920 World Series was a memorable one. Who won it? A clue: It was this team's first Series appearance.

24. Name the Cleveland outfielder who hit the first Series grand slam home run in the 5th game in 1920.

25. Name the Cleveland pitcher who, in the same game, became the first pitcher to hit a World Series home run.

26. Who was the Cleveland second baseman who, still in the same game, executed the only unassisted triple play in Series history?

27. Finally, name the Cleveland pitcher who got three wins in the Series, including victories in the first and last games.

28. The leading hitters in both the AL and the NL played in the same city in 1920. Can you name them?

29. Can you name the brothers, both outfielders, who played against each other in the World Series for three straight years, 1921–1923?

30. Name the Giant outfielder who hit an inside-the-park home run in the first game of the 1923 Series, the first Series game played at the new Yankee Stadium.

31. The 1927 Yankees are considered one of the greatest teams of all time. Who did they beat in the Series that year?

32. What Yankee regular had the highest batting average in that Series?

33. Who was the manager of the 1927 Yankees?

34. The 1927 Yankees had six pitchers with ten or more wins, but only one with more than 20. Who was he?

35. Who was the Philadelphia Athletics pitcher who set a new

Series record when he struck out 13 Chicago Cubs in the first game of the 1929 Series?

36. The Athletics won that 1929 Series but lost two years later to the Cardinals in seven games. Name the St. Louis outfielder who got 12 hits in the 1931 Series, batting .500 as his team won in seven.

37. Who was the Chicago Cub pitcher against whom Babe Ruth hit his famous "called shot" home run in the 1932 Series?

38. Did the Yankees sweep that Series in four games?

39. Did Babe Ruth hit two home runs in the final game?

40. Name the New York Giant outfielder who homered in the first and last games of the 1933 Series to lead his team to a Series win over the Senators.

41. How many pitchers on that 1933 Giant team won 20 or more games?

42. Who was the manager of the 1933 Giants? Clue: He was the last National Leaguer to hit .400 for a season.

43. Name the two brothers who each won two games for the winning team in the 1934 Series.

44. What was their team's nickname?

45. Who was their manager? A clue: He was also their second baseman.

46. Who did they beat in that 1934 Series?

47. The team that lost the Series in 1934 came back to win in 1935. What Hall of Famer drove in the Series-winning run in the last inning of the final 1935 game?

48. Give yourself extra credit if you know the name of the Hall of Fame catcher who scored that run.

49. The Yankees won four straight World Series from 1936 through 1939. What great Yankee outfielder made his Series debut in 1936, batting .346 in six games against the Giants?

50. Who was the Yankees' manager during that streak?

51. What Yankee pitcher won the most Series games during those four years?

52. What team finally, in 1942, beat the Yankees in a World Series, the Yankees' first Series loss after eight victories beginning in 1927?

53. Who hit the two-run home run in the 9th inning of the final game to seal New York's defeat?

54. Who was the winning pitcher in the first World Series game played after World War II?

55. Did his team win the Series?

56. How many Series did the Yankees win in a row after Casey Stengel became their manager in 1949?

57. How many seasons did Stengel win 100 or more games with the Yankees?

58. Where did Stengel's Yankees finish in 1954?

59. What Yankee pitcher won the most World Series games between 1949 and 1953?

60. In those same five years, what Yankee hit home runs in three consecutive World Series games?

61. Name the Yankee second baseman who led the team with eight RBIs in the 1953 Series.

62. Did any Yankees other than Mickey Mantle hit a grand slam home run during those five Series?

63. The Yankees stole only six bases in all five of those Series combined. Three of them were stolen by their shortstop. Who was he?

64. The Cleveland team that took the 1954 AL pennant had five pitchers who combined for 93 victories. How many of the five can you name?

65. How did that Cleveland team do in the Series?

66. Who was the winning pitcher in the last game when the Dodgers finally won their first World Series in 1955, beating the Yankees in seven games?

67. Who was the Dodger leftfielder who saved that final game with a spectacular running catch in the 6th inning?

68. Who hit the ball he caught?

69. Can you name the Dodger outfielder who hit four home runs in that Series?

70. When the Yankees turned the tables on Brooklyn in 1956 with a seven-game Series victory, who was the winning pitcher in the final game?

71. Name the Yankee righthander who turned in the only perfect game in Series history, in Game 5 of that 1956 Series.

72. Who was the losing pitcher for Brooklyn that day?

73. Name the Milwaukee Brave righthander who won three Series games against the Yankees in 1957, helping his team to a seven-game win.

74. Who was the winning pitcher in the first World Series game played on the West Coast?

75. Who were the managers of the two teams in the 1959 Series?

76. Mickey Mantle drove in 11 runs for the Yankees in the 1960 World Series against Pittsburgh. Is that a Series record?

77. Name the Pirate second baseman who hit the winning home run for Pittsburgh in the last of the 9th in the 7th game in 1960.

78. What Yankee pitcher surrendered that home run?

79. Who was the manager of the 1960 Pirates?

80. The 1961 Yankees had six players who each hit more than 20 home runs. How many can you name?

81. Did that team win the World Series?

82. How many of the six hit home runs in the 1961 Series?

83. When the Yankees and Dodgers met in the 1963 Series, former Yankee Bill Skowron was now playing first for the Dodgers. Who replaced him at first base for the Yankees?

84. The Dodgers handled the Yankees in four straight games that year, needing only four pitchers to win the Series. How many of the four pitchers who appeared in the 1963 Series for Los Angeles can you name?

85. An era ended in 1964: the Yankees' last Series appearance until 1977. Though they lost in seven to St. Louis, one Yankee, a free-spirited righthander who later became a noted author, had a fine Series with two wins. Who was he?

86. Who managed the Cardinal team that won that Series?

87. Who managed the Yankee team that lost it?

88. Name the Baltimore Oriole outfielder whose solo home run

in the 4th inning of the 4th and final game of the 1966 Series against the Dodgers produced the game's only score.

89. Who managed that Oriole team?

90. The 1967 and 1968 Series were dominated by two pitchers, a National League righthander who posted three wins in 1967 and an American League lefthander who won three in 1968. Who were they?

91. Were the 1969 Mets the first expansion team to win a Series?

92. Who was their manager?

93. How many 20-game winners did they have?

94. Name the two Mets who homered in the 5th and final game of the 1969 Series against the Orioles.

95. Who was the owner of the Oakland team that won three straight World Series in 1972, 1973 and 1974?

96. Who managed those Oakland teams?

97. What Oakland player hit the most World Series home runs during those three years combined?

98. What member of the Cincinnati Reds' "Big Red Machine" delivered the 9th-inning single that won the 7th game of the 1975 Series against the Red Sox?

99. How long had it been since the Reds had won the Series?

100. What Boston pitcher posted two complete-game wins during that Series?

101. Who was the Big Red Machine's manager?

102. Name the opposing catchers who both delivered great offensive performances in the 1976 Series.

103. The Yankees returned to Series action with back-to-back six game wins against Los Angeles in 1977 and 1978. Who managed the Yankee and Dodger teams in those Series?

104. How many players hit at least three home runs in either of those Series?

105. What Yankee pitcher posted two complete-game wins in the 1977 Series?

106. Who was the Yankee third baseman whose spectacular defensive play was a major factor, especially in 1978?

107. What team won the first World Series in their history in 1980?

108. Who was the relief pitcher who recorded the crucial save in the final Series game that year?

109. What Dodger outfielder drove in five runs in the final game of the 1981 Series as Los Angeles got some revenge against the Yankees for 1977 and 1978 with a six-game Series win?

110. Who was the winning pitcher in the 7th and final game of the 1982 Series won by St. Louis over Milwaukee?

111. Who was the winning pitcher in the 7th and final game of the 1985 Series won by Kansas City over St. Louis?

112. Who managed that Kansas City team?

113. Name the Red Sox player whose crucial error in the 6th game of the 1986 Series helped the Mets stage a miraculous comeback?

114. Which Met player drove in the most runs in that Series?

115. Name the Dodger player who, even though hobbled by injuries, delivered a crucial pinch hit home run in the first

game of the 1988 Series, starting Los Angeles on their way to a five-game win over Oakland.

116. Name the Dodger pitcher who posted two complete-game wins in that Series.

117. Who was the Minnesota Twin pitcher who delivered a ten-inning complete game shutout in the 7th game of the 1991 Series as the Twins beat Atlanta?

118. Name the Toronto outfielder whose two-run 11th-inning double in Game 6 gave Toronto their 1992 Series win over the Braves.

119. Who was the Toronto lefthander who posted two wins in that Series?

120. Name the Toronto outfielder whose three-run home run in the bottom of the 9th inning of Game 6 in 1993 gave the Blue Jays their second straight World Series victory.

121. Who was named the Most Valuable Player of the 1993 World Series?

Brothers

Many sets of brothers have played with and against each other in the major leagues. Here are some questions about the accomplishments of baseball-playing brothers.

1. Name the brothers who hit the most career home runs.

2. Did the same set of brothers drive in the most career runs?

3. Name the two sets of pitching brothers who each won more than 500 games in their careers.

4. Name the only two sets of brothers who combined for more than 5,000 hits.

5. What teammate brothers had the most home runs in a season?

6. What set of teammate brothers won the most combined games pitching in one season?

7. Who were the first pitching brothers who each won at least 20 games in a season?

8. Who were the only brothers who pitched a combined shutout in the major leagues?

A Pitching Quiz

1. Name the two pitchers who appeared in more than 1,000 major league games.

2. What pitcher active since World War II has the most career wins?

3. Can you name the four pitchers ahead of him on the all-time win list?

4. Who gave up the most grand slam home runs in his career?

5. Of the 12 pitchers who pitched more than 5,000 innings, six were active since World War II. How many can you name?

6. Only one pitcher recorded more than 100 shutouts. Who was he?

7. Only one pitcher gave up more than 2,000 bases on balls. Who was he?

8. Four pitchers won more than 100 games pitching in relief. How many members of this talented quartet can you name?

9. What pitcher recorded the most strikeouts in a single season?

10. Who pitched in the most games in a single season?

11. Since World War II, who had the best earned run average for a single season?

12. Who recorded the most shutouts in a single season?

13. Who recorded the most shutouts in a single season since World War II?

14. What pitcher hit the most batters in his career?

15. What pitcher led the league in lowest earned run average the most seasons?

16. What pitcher led the league in lowest earned run average the most consecutive seasons?

17. You're an expert if you can name the pitcher who pitched the most consecutive innings without issuing a walk.

18. Who was the last AL pitcher to win 30 games in a season?

19. Who was the last before him?

20. Who was the last NL pitcher to win 30 games in a season?

21. What is the 20th-century record for wins in a season?

22. What pitcher led the league in wins the most times?

23. What pitcher won 20 or more games the most times?

24. Who won the most games for a last-place team?

25. Since 1930, has any lefthander beside Lefty Grove won 30 or more games in a season?

26. Who was the last Yankee pitcher to win 25 or more games in a season?

27. Who was the last Dodger pitcher to win 25 or more games in a season?

28. Five pitchers won 100 or more games in each league. How many can you name?

29. Who was the last pitcher to start both games of a double-header?

30. How did he do?

31. If you go way back you might know who was the only pitcher to pitch two complete-game shutouts on the same day.

32. Who pitched the first no-hitter for an expansion team?

33. Who pitched the last no-hitter on opening day?

34. Who has the most career no-hitters?

35. What pitcher retired the most batters in a row?

36. What Cardinal player got a double to end the streak at 41?

37. What pitcher recorded the most consecutive wins?

38. Did any pitcher ever win the Cy Young Award in both leagues?

39. Who is the only NL pitcher to hit two grand slam home runs in a game?

40. How many other National League players, including non-pitchers, have hit two grand slams in a game?

41. Who pitched the most innings in a single game?

42. What twentieth-century pitcher with at least 200 career decisions has the highest winning percentage?

43. What pitcher recorded the most consecutive strikeouts in a game?

44. What pitcher recorded the most consecutive 200-strikeout seasons?

Most Valuable Player/
Cy Young Award Winners

1. Can you name all five American Leaguers who won the Most Valuable Player title two years in a row?

2. How many National Leaguers did this?

3. Who were the first players in each league to be named MVP?

4. Since 1956, pitchers have had their own Cy Young award, but sometimes pitchers have such great seasons that they are considered for the MVP award as well. Who were the last pitchers in each league to win the MVP?

5. In 1956, when the Cy Young award was inaugurated, there was only one award for both leagues—who won that first Cy Young?

6. Pitchers won the American League MVP award once in the 1950s, once in the 1960s and once in the 1970s. Can you name these three pitchers?

7. Has a rookie player ever won the MVP award?

8. What player was MVP in both leagues?

9. Who was the oldest MVP?

10. Who was the youngest MVP?

11. Name the two National League pitchers who won the MVP award during the 1950s, and the two who won it during the 1960s.

12. When was the last time that three different players from the same team won the American League MVP award in three consecutive years?

13. Was that the only time this happened in the American League?

14. When was the last time that three different players on the same team won three consecutive National League MVPs?

15. Was this the only time this happened in NL history?

16. Who was the first American League pitcher to win a Cy Young award?

17. Has there ever been a four-time Cy Young winner?

18. Who was the only rookie pitcher to win the Cy Young award?

Managers

Some of baseball's most colorful personalities have been managers. Here's a quick test of your knowledge of the men who make the decisions.

1. In each league, who managed for the most seasons?

2. Did these men win the most pennants as managers in their respective leagues?

3. Can you name the two managers who each won the World Series a record seven times?

4. Two managers won pennants with three different teams. Can you name them?

5. Who managed for the most years without winning a pennant?

6. What manager has the highest career winning percentage?

7. Who was the last player-manager to win a pennant?

8. In the twentieth century, has a pitcher ever won a pennant as a player-manager?

Nicknames

Baseball has produced some great nicknames. Here are the nicknames of more than 100 major leaguers—see how many you can identify with the help of the clues provided:

1. "Scoops." A Hall of Famer, this Pirate outfielder led the NL in stolen bases ten times between 1913 and 1925.

2. "Highpockets." A Hall of Famer, this first baseman drove in over a hundred runs in each of four consecutive seasons with the New York Giants from 1921 to 1924.

3. "The Big Cat." This great first baseman batted over .300 in his first nine major league seasons, and led or tied for the NL lead in home runs four times between 1939 and 1948.

4. "Pudge." One of the few catchers to have a playing career in the major leagues of more than 20 years.

5. "Mex." This Cardinal first baseman led the NL with a .344 average and 116 RBIs in 1979. In 1986 he helped the Mets win their second world championship.

6. "Old Aches and Pains." This White Sox shortstop led the AL with a .388 batting average in 1936, and again with a .328 average in 1943. He's one of the few major leaguers who played 20 years with the same team.

7. "Say Hey." This Hall of Famer's 660 home runs are third all-time behind only Hank Aaron and Babe Ruth.

8. "The Mighty Mite." This diminutive second baseman had a good playing career between 1904 and 1916, but is best remembered today for the six pennants he won as manager of the Yankees during the 1920s.

9. "The Peerless Leader." This Hall of Fame playing manager was just that for the Chicago Cubs in the early years of this century.

10. "Slug." A Hall of Famer, this Detroit Tiger outfielder never got to play in a World Series during his 17-year career, but led the AL in batting four times in the 1920s. He batted over .300 for 12 consecutive seasons beginning in 1919.

11. "Scooter." Shortstop on the great Yankee teams of the early 1950s, and then a baseball broadcaster for more than three decades, he was named the AL's Most Valuable Player in 1950 when he collected 200 hits and batted .324.

12. "The Duke of Tralee." A Hall of Fame catcher and playing manager from major league baseball's early days, he also played the outfield and every infield position at one time or another.

13. "Mad Dog." He batted .305 during a 15-year career and led the NL in hitting four times between 1975 and 1983, twice with the Cubs and twice with the Pirates.

14. "The Bull." Earning his nickname with his 6′1″, 220-lb. physique, this slugger accumulated 307 home runs in a 15-year career, 1970–1984. His 120 RBIs for the Phillies led the NL in 1975.

15. "Penguin." This Dodger third baseman with the unorthodox gait never hit .300, but did produce 316 home runs in his 17-year career.

16. "Roadrunner." He earned his nickname with seasons like 1974 when he led the NL with a .353 average, 214 hits and 17 triples.

17. "Stonewall." This Hall of Famer played his whole career with the New York Giants. A shortstop, he batted over .300 six times between 1924 and 1935.

18. "Ducky." This Hall of Famer batted .324 for 17 seasons between 1932 and 1948. In 1937 he had the kind of year players dream about when he led the NL with a .374 batting average, 237 hits, 31 home runs, 111 runs scored and 154 runs batted in.

19. "Little Napoleon." The indomitable manager of the New York Giants from 1902 to 1932, he led his team to ten pennants during that period.

20. "Beauty." A shortstop, he teamed with second baseman Frankie Frisch on John McGraw's New York Giant teams in the early 1920s.

21. "The Tall Tactician." His mediocre playing career ended in 1896, but he's well remembered today for managing the Philadelphia Athletics for 50 years beginning in 1901. Through longevity, he both won and lost more games than any other manager in major league history.

22. "The Cobra." A hard-hitting Pittsburgh outfielder, his .338 and .334 batting averages led the NL in 1977 and 1978.

23. "The Mechanical Man." A hitting machine, this Tiger second baseman collected 200 or more hits seven times in his Hall of Fame career.

24. "Mr. October." Sixth on the all-time home run list with 563 in his 21-year career, this outfielder earned his nickname with a host of impressive World Series totals including a .357 batting average, 10 home runs and 24 RBIs in 27 World Series games.

25. "Stretch." This tall first baseman, a Hall of Famer, led the NL in both home runs and RBIs in two consecutive years, 1968 and 1969.

26. "Cha-Cha." This Giant first baseman's 46 home runs and 142 RBIs led the NL in 1961.

27. "Wee Willie." This 5′4.5″ Hall of Fame outfielder collected over 200 hits in eight consecutive seasons for Baltimore and Brooklyn in the National League between 1894 and 1901.

28. "Old Reliable." This native of Massillon, Ohio was a steady outfield performer for the Yankees in the years before and after World War II. He scored 138 runs to lead the AL in 1948.

29. "Mandrake the Magician." A mainstay of the New York Giants teams during their last decade in New York, this outfielder had a .296 career batting average and led the NL with 212 hits in 1954.

30. "Sliding Billy." This outfielder's 14-year playing career ended in 1901; 60 years later he was elected to the Hall of Fame. He stole over 100 bases three times, and his .344 lifetime batting average is 7th on the all-time list.

31. "Sunny Jim." A hard-hitting Cardinal first baseman, he drove in over 100 runs for six straight years, 1924–1929.

32. "The Fordham Flash." Playing for the Giants and Cardinals, this Hall of Famer batted .316 for his 19-year career and led the NL in stolen bases three times.

33. "Rajah." This Hall of Fame infielder batted over .400 three times and collected over 200 hits seven times in his 23-year career, which began in 1915. His .358 lifetime batting average is topped only by Ty Cobb's .367.

34. "Rabbit." A Hall of Famer, he played over 2,000 games at

shortstop for five teams during a 23-year career, 1912–1935, which both began and ended with the Boston Braves.

35. "The Little Colonel." Leader of the great Dodger teams of the 1940s and 1950s, he played in 140 or more games during 13 seasons between 1941 and 1956—with time out for World War II—and was elected to the Hall of Fame in 1984.

36. "The Kentucky Colonel." He played centerfield, with Babe Ruth in right, for the great Yankee teams of the late 1920s and early 1930s.

37. "Poosh 'Em Up." The Yankees' second baseman during the glory days of Babe Ruth, he batted over .300 four consecutive years, 1927–1930. He earned his nickname for his uncanny ability to advance baserunners to scoring position.

38. "The Wild Hoss of the Osage." A leader of the Cardinals' "Gas House Gang" in the 1930s, his .418 World Series batting average, compiled in 15 Series games, is the highest in history.

39. "The Iron Horse." Among many records, he led the AL in runs batted in five times between 1927 and 1934.

40. "Gabby." A Hall of Fame catcher with the Chicago Cubs for 19 seasons between 1922 and 1940, he hit .344 in 1935, and .354 in 1937.

41. "Slats." A slick-fielding shortstop, he made it to the World Series four times with the Cardinals during the 1940s.

42. "Hondo." This 6'7" Washington Senator led the AL with 44 home runs in both 1968 and 1970.

43. "The Lip." Shortstop on some of the famous St. Louis Cardinal "Gashouse Gang" teams of the 1930s, he went on to greater fame as a manager once his playing days were over.

44. "Skoonj." This Dodger outfielder batted over .300 five times in his 15-year career, and led the NL with a .344 average in 1953.

45. "Hawk." A first baseman-outfielder, his 109 RBIs for Boston led the AL in 1968.

46. "The Beast." A Hall of Fame first baseman, in the top ten all-time both with 534 home runs and 1,921 runs batted in.

47. "Le Grande Orange." This solid-hitting outfielder-first baseman-designated hitter played in almost 3,000 games during a 23-year career which ended in 1985.

48. "Tug." This lefthander saved 180 games for the Mets and Phillies between 1965 and 1984.

49. "Mudcat." Pitching for the pennant-winning Twins, he led the AL in victories in 1965 with a 21–7 record, and picked up two more wins in the Series as the Twins lost to the Dodgers in seven games.

50. "Little Poison" and "Big Poison." These brothers, both Hall of Famers, starred in the Pittsburgh outfield during the 1930s. In their combined 38 major league seasons, they batted over .300 25 times.

51. "Preacher." A consistent lefthander best remembered for his years in Brooklyn, he led the NL in winning percentage with 15–6 and 22–3 records for the 1949 and 1951 Dodgers.

52. "Lefty." He led the NL in wins four times betwen 1972 and 1982. His 4,136 career strikeout mark is second only to Nolan Ryan's.

53. "The Barber." Remembered as a tough competitor, he led the NL in wins with a 23–6 record for the pennant-winning 1951 Giants.

54. "Old Hoss." Compiling a .336 average during his 14-year playing career, the Cubs couldn't blame this outfielder for their World Series losses in 1929 and 1932. He hit .378 during the nine games of those series, of which the Cubs won only one.

55. "Moose." This dependable first baseman played for five teams during his 14-year career, 1954–1967, but is best remembered for his time with seven Yankee pennant winners. His eight World Series home runs puts him 7th on the all-time list in that category.

56. "Iron Man." This Hall of Famer earned his nickname by occasionally pitching and completing both games of a double-header. He led the NL in wins with 31–20 and 35–8 records for the 1903 and 1904 New York Giants.

57. "The Gay Castillion." This free-spirited Yankee lefthander led the AL in wins with 26 in 1934 and 21 in 1937. In seven World Series starts, he compiled a flawless 6–0 mark, and was elected to the Hall of Fame in 1972.

58. "The Flying Dutchman." One of the great legends of baseball's early years, this Pirate shortstop led the NL in hitting eight times between 1900 and 1911.

59. "Catfish." This consistent lefthander won at least 21 games for five consecutive years from 1971 through 1975 and led the AL in wins twice during that period. His 224–166 record earned him admission to the Hall of Fame in 1987.

60. "Knucksie." This righthanded knuckleballer won 318 games during a 24-year career from 1964 through 1987. He led the NL in wins for the 1974 and 1979 Braves with 20–13 and 21–20 records.

61. "The Chairman of the Board." The Hall of Fame lefthander led the AL in wins three times between 1955 and 1963. He holds a host of all-time World Series records including most

wins, 10; losses, 8; games started, 22; innings pitched, 146; strikeouts, 94; and walks, 34.

62. "Yo-Yo." This relief pitcher had his best season with the 1961 Yankees when he finished with 15 wins and 29 saves, often completing games started by Whitey Ford.

63. "Manito." One of the dominant pitchers of the 1960s, this Hall of Famer won 191 games for the San Francisco Giants during that decade.

64. "The Arkansas Humming Bird." He led the NL in wins with a 22–6 record with the pennant-winning 1932 Chicago Cubs.

65. "Twinkletoes." A Yankee outfielder for his entire, though brief career—nine seasons between 1934 and 1942—he batted over .300 in five of those years, and played in the World Series in six of them.

66. "Ol' Stubblebeard." This Hall of Famer had a 270–212 record over 19 seasons, 1916–1934. He had five 20-plus winning seasons, and is remembered as the last legal spitball pitcher in the majors.

67. "Steady Eddie." A productive lefthander known for his off-speed deliveries, he won 80 games for the Yankees' five consecutive World Championship teams between 1949 and 1953.

68. "The Springfield Rifle." This native of West Springfield, Mass., won 92 games for the Yankees' five consecutive World Championship teams, 1949–1953, and picked up five more wins in those World Series.

69. "The Brat." A solid second baseman for five teams during his 11-year career, he had a sharp batting eye. Out of eight major league seasons in which he appeared in over 100 games, he led the NL in bases on balls three times.

70. "The Splendid Splinter." The last major leaguer to bat over

.400 for a season, he compiled a .406 mark for the 1941 Red Sox.

71. "Firpo." One of the first great relief specialists, this Washington Senator led the AL in appearances by a pitcher six times between 1924 and 1932.

72. "The Terminator." One of contemporary baseball's best relief pitchers, he led the AL in saves with 34 for Toronto in 1987.

73. "Three Finger." This Hall of Famer's 2.06 career ERA is third best all-time. He won 20 or more games in six consecutive seasons for the Chicago Cubs beginning in 1906.

74. "The Wizard." Universally acclaimed as the greatest shortstop of his generation, he batted over .300 for the first time in his 10th major league season.

75. "Rapid Robert." This Hall of Famer pitched for the Cleveland Indians for 18 seasons between 1936 and 1956. He won 20 or more games six times, and in each of those seasons led the AL in wins.

76. "Goose." One of the great relief pitchers of recent decades, he led the AL in saves three times between 1974 and 1980.

77. "Prince Hal." This lefthander won 118 games for the Detroit Tigers in a five-year span, 1944–1948; in four of those five seasons he led the AL in victories. His career 207–150 mark earned him belated admission to the Hall of Fame 37 years after he retired in 1955.

78. "The Hoosier Thunderbolt." This Hall of Famer won 246 games between 1889 and 1898 including four years with more than 30 wins.

79. "The Little Steam Engine." His playing career ended in 1892, but his 361 lifetime wins, 6th on the all-time list, got him elected to the Hall of Fame in 1965.

80. "Gus." This Hall of Famer won 300 games for three AL teams between 1939 and 1963. He tied for the AL lead in wins with a 23–11 record for the 1954 Indians, and led the AL with a 22–10 mark for the 1959 White Sox, the only two non-Yankee pennant-winners in the decade.

81. "Gator." The best pitcher in baseball in 1978, the year he led the AL in victories with a 25–3 record, in ERA at a phenomenal 1.74, and pitched nine shutouts for the pennant-winning Yankees.

82. "Sudden Sam." This hard-throwing Cleveland Indian left-hander led the AL in strikeouts five times between 1965 and 1970.

83. "The People's Cherce." He played for three AL teams before moving in 1939 to Brooklyn, where he earned his nickname as a popular outfielder during the next nine seasons. His .357 batting average led the NL in 1944.

84. "The Gray Eagle." He batted .344, 7th all-time, for his 22-year career, which ended in 1928. His 793 doubles are the most in major league history.

85. "The Walking Man." This third baseman walked 1,614 times, 7th highest all-time, during his 18-year career. He led the AL in bases on balls six times between 1950 and 1960.

86. "Dizzy." This Hall of Famer compiled a 150–83 record in an injury-shortened 12-year career that included 30–7 and 28–12 seasons for the 1934 and 1935 Cardinals.

87. "The Big Train." His 110 career shutouts top the all-time list. He won 416 games during his 21-year Hall of Fame career, and led the AL in victories six times between 1913 and 1924.

88. "The Big Bear." A prominent member of the great Cleveland pitching staffs of the 1950s, he won 79 games from 1951 through 1954, the year his 2.64 ERA led the AL.

89. "Country." This Hall of Famer batted exactly .300 for 19 seasons between 1938 and 1959—2,383 hits in 7,946 times at bat. His 130 RBIs led the NL in 1946.

90. "Zorro." A fine shortstop, he moved with the Senators to Minnesota after the 1960 season. He helped the Twins to their 1965 pennant when he led the AL in doubles, triples and runs scored.

91. "Mose." He won exactly 300 games during his 17-year Hall of Fame career, and led the AL in ERA nine times between 1926 and 1939.

92. "Big Six." One of the pitching legends of baseball's early years, this Hall of Famer won 30 or more games four times, and is among the all-time leaders in wins, 373; career ERA, 2.13; and shutouts, 80.

93. "Dazzy." This Hall of Famer led the NL in wins in consecutive seasons with 28–6 and 22–9 records for the 1924 and 1925 Dodgers. He finished his 16-year career with a 197–140 mark.

94. "The Pride of Havana." A consistent righthander who won 193 major league games between 1918 and 1935, his 27–8 record with Cincinnati led the NL in victories in 1923.

95. "The Old Professor." He played the outfield and batted .284 for five NL teams during a 14-year playing career which ended in 1925. He earned enduring fame as manager of the Yankees from 1949 through 1960, including the record streak of five consecutive World Championships, 1949–1953.

96. "Bullet Joe." This productive righthander compiled a 194–183 mark over 17 seasons. In his only 20-plus winning year, he was 26–7 for the 1922 Yankees.

97. "Fireman." This crafty righthander won 73 games as a relief

pitcher for the Yankees between 1934 and 1946 including six seasons in which he led the AL in wins by a reliever.

98. "Schoolboy." A capable righthander, he won 158 games during his 15-year career, including a 24–8 season with the pennant-winning 1934 Detroit Tigers.

99. "The Meal Ticket." Baseball's dominant pitcher from 1933 through 1937—a five-year span during which this Hall of Famer collected 115 wins for the New York Giants.

100. "The Kitten." This stylish lefthander is best remembered today for having pitched 12 perfect innings for Pittsburgh against Milwaukee on May 26, 1959, only to lose the no-hitter and the game in the 13th.

101. "The Hat." Traded from the Cardinals to the Phillies after ten games of the 1947 season, he then batted .363 for the year to become the only player to win an NL batting title while splitting a season between two teams.

102. "Pie." He batted .320 during his 17-year Hall of Fame career, 1920–1937, as a third baseman for the Pittsburgh Pirates.

103. "Oisk." A prominent member of five pennant-winning Dodger pitching staffs, this righthander was 20–6 in 1953, his best season.

104. "Big Six." He helped pitch the Detroit Tigers to consecutive pennants in 1934 and 1935 with 15–7 and 18–7 records.

105. "Daddy Wags." A stylish outfielder, he hit more than 20 home runs for six consecutive years, three with the Angels, and three with the Indians, beginning in 1961.

106. "No-Neck." A productive outfielder with several teams, he batted .270 for his ten major league seasons, and led the AL with ten pinch hits for the 1975 Yankees in his final year.

107. "Dr. Strangeglove." As his nickname indicates, fielding wasn't the strong suit of this hard-hitting first baseman. He led the NL with 121 RBIs for the 1961 Pirates, then topped the AL with 118 for the 1963 Red Sox.

Answers

A True–False Baseball History Quiz

1. True. 111 in 1952.

2. False. Spahn won his only Cy Young in 1957. Sandy Koufax, in 1965 and 1966, was the first back-to-back Cy Young winner.

3. False. Mathewson's 373 wins ties him with Grover Cleveland Alexander for third place—Walter Johnson is second to Young with 416 wins.

4. True. Seaver won 311 while Grove and Wynn each won 300.

5. False. Baltimore won their playoff series from Minnesota.

6. False. Bob Meusel's 33 led the AL in 1925.

7. False. Frank Howard was, with 44 in 1970.

8. False. Mike Schmidt was, 1974–1976.

9. False. Dave Kingman's 48 led the NL in 1979, and Andre Dawson's 49 was tops in 1987.

10. False. San Francisco's Orlando Cepeda's 46 led the NL in 1961.

11. True, with 32 in 1973.

12. True, with 47 in 1964 and 52 in 1965.

13. False. Jackie Jensen was, with 122 in 1958 and 112 in 1959.

14. False. Roger Maris was, with 112 in 1960 and 142 in 1961.

15. True.

16. False. Don Mattingly led the AL with 145 RBIs in 1985.

17. False. Hack Wilson's 190 for the 1930 Chicago Cubs is the all-time RBI record.

18. False. Stan Musial led the NL with a .376 average in 1948.

19. True.

20. True.

21. False. Carl Yastrzemski's .301 in 1968 is the lowest ever to lead the AL.

22. False. George Brett's .390 in 1980 has been tops in the AL since 1941.

23. False. New York Giant Bill Terry was the last with a .401 average in 1930.

24. True.

25. False. He led the NL with a .328 average in 1956, and again with a .355 average in 1959.

26. False. St. Louis' Rogers Hornsby batted .424 in 1924 while Sisler's best was .420 in 1922.

27. True, .357 in 1967.

28. False. Detroit's Norm Cash led the AL with a .361 average in 1961.

29. False. Alex Johnson of the Angels led the AL with a .329 average in 1970.

30. False. George Brett led the AL with a .333 average in 1976 and with a .329 average in 1990.

31. True.

32. True.

33. True.

34. False. Wrigley seats 38,710 while Fenway Park in Boston seats 34,142.

35. False. In 1979, Pittsburgh's Willie Stargell and St. Louis' Keith Hernandez tied for the NL MVP award.

36. False. Dodger Maury Wills was the first—in 1962.

37. True—in 1971.

38. False. No Senator ever won the award.

39. False. New York Giant pitcher Carl Hubbell was the first two-time winner, 1933 and 1936.

40. True—1943, 1946 and 1948.

41. True—1932 and 1933.

42. False. Elston Howard, 1963, and Thurman Munson, 1976.

43. False. Four were winners. Johnny Bench (1970 and 1972), Pete Rose (1973), Joe Morgan (1975 and 1976) and George Foster (1977).

44. True—1960–1961.

45. False. Three won the award—Tom Seaver, 1967, Jon Matlack, 1972, and Dwight Gooden, 1984.

46. True.

47. False. The Dodgers had four from 1979 to 1982—Rick Sutcliffe, Steve Howe, Fernando Valenzuela and Steve Sax.

48. True. Brooks Robinson, Frank Robinson, Jackie Robinson and Wilbert Robinson.

49. False. It was played at Chicago's Comiskey Park in 1933. The AL won 4–2.

50. False. Len Barker pitched one for Cleveland against Toronto in 1981. The final score was 3–0.

51. True. Al Lopez managed the 1954 Cleveland Indians and the 1959 Chicago White Sox.

52. False. Pittsburgh's Fred Clarke won pennants in 1901, 1902 and 1903.

53. True. Weaver led the Orioles to AL pennants in 1969, 1970 and 1971.

54. False. Cincinnati's Sparky Anderson won in 1975 and 1976.

55. False. Bill Melton led the AL in home runs with 33 in 1971.

56. False. Cleveland's Al Rosen led the AL with 37 home runs in 1950 and 43 in 1953, while the Indians' Larry Doby did the same with 32 in 1952 and 32 again in 1954.

57. True, with 43 in 1956.

58. True.

59. False. Snider led the NL with 136 in 1955, but Roy Campanella also did, with 142 in 1953.

60. False. Monte Irvin was, with 121 in 1951.

61. True. Fielder's numbers were 132 in 1990, 133 in 1991 and 124 in 1992.

62. False. Medwick did this in 1936–1938, but the last NL player to do it was Cincinnati's George Foster with 121 in 1976, 149 in 1977 and 120 in 1978.

63. True.

64. False. Tony Armas led the AL with 123 in 1984.

65. False. Bell never won a batting title. John Olerud became the first Toronto player to do so with a .363 average in 1993.

66. False. Seattle's Edgar Martinez led the AL with a .343 average in 1992.

67. True.

68. True.

69. False. Kirby Puckett led the AL with a .339 average in 1989.

70. False. Gary Sheffield led the NL with a .330 average in 1992.

71. True.

72. False. The Rangers' Julio Franco led the AL with a .341 average in 1991.

73. False. Jim Lonborg won in 1967.

74. False. Lyle won in 1977, but Ron Guidry won in 1978.

75. False. Mike Marshall won in 1974.

76. True.

77. False. The Astros' Mike Scott won in 1986.

78. True.

79. False. Doug Drabek won in 1990.

80. False. Dodger Don Newcombe won in 1949.

81. False. Brooklyn's Jackie Robinson won the award as a first baseman in 1947.

82. False. Allison won in 1959, but Washington outfielder Albie Pearson won in 1958.

83. True.

84. False. Atlanta catcher Earl Williams won in 1971.

85. True.

86. False. Frank Robinson won in 1956.

87. True.

88. False. Yankee Reggie Jackson was selected in 1993, his first year of eligibility.

89. True.

90. True.

91. False. Ryan's first four no-hitters were as a California Angel, the fifth for Houston and the last two for Texas.

92. True. Rose batted 14,053 times. Next on the list is Hank Aaron with 12,364.

93. False. Veterans Stadium seats 62,383, less than the Colorado Rockies' Mile High Stadium with 76,100.

94. False. Fenway Park is 390 feet to center, but Dodger Stadium is only 395.

95. False. Yankee Rudy May led the AL with a 2.47 ERA in 1980. Gooden's league-leading year was 1985 with 1.53.

96. True, 1.93 in 1990.

97. False. Ted Williams, tied for 10th with 521, was in the majors before World War II.

98. False. Bert Blyleven with 60 shutouts, is 9th on the list. Spahn had 63, Ryan and Seaver 61 each.

99. True. Cobb tops the runs list with 2,245. Rose is 4th with 2,165.

100. True. Yaz got 3,419 hits, 7th on the all-time list. Mays is 9th with 3,283.

World Series History

1. Yes, three times. In 1966, the Orioles swept the Los Angeles Dodgers; in 1989 the Athletics swept the San Francisco Giants; in 1990 the Reds swept the Athletics.

2. The Dodgers, 18 times.

3. Yogi Berra. Berra played on the Yankees Series winners in 1947, 1949–1953, 1956, 1958 and 1961–1962.

4. Eddie Collins and Lou Brock with 14 stolen bases. Collins played for two American League teams, Philadelphia in 1910, 1911, 1913 and 1914, and Chicago in 1917 and 1919. Brock appeared with the Cardinals in 1964, 1967 and 1968.

5. October 13, 1971 at Pittsburgh—Pittsburgh vs. Baltimore.

6. Los Angeles, October 6, 1959—Los Angeles vs. Chicago. The crowd was 92,706.

7. No. Paul Molitor of Milwaukee got his record five hits in the first game of the 1982 Series against St. Louis.

8. Reggie Jackson, Yankees, 1977. Ruth did it twice, in 1926 and 1928.

9. Honus Wagner, Pittsburgh, 1909; Willie Davis, Los Angeles, 1965; Lou Brock, St. Louis, twice—1967 and 1968.

10. Robin Yount, Milwaukee, first and fifth games, 1982.

11. Bob Gibson, St. Louis, 1968—17 strikeouts.

12. Bobby Richardson, New York Yankees, 6 in 1960.

13. Monte Irvin, New York Giants, 1951; Jackie Robinson, Brooklyn Dodgers, 1955; and Tim McCarver, St. Louis Cardinals, 1964.

14. Babe Ruth, New York Yankees, .625 in 1928.

15. Reggie Jackson, New York Yankees, 5 in 1977.

16. Sandy Koufax, Los Angeles Dodgers, 23 in 1963.

17. Bob Gibson, St. Louis Cardinals, 35 in 7 games, 1968.

18. George Selkirk, Elston Howard, Roger Maris, Jim Mason and Bob Watson.

19. Lefty Gomez, New York Yankees, 6.

20. Grover Cleveland Alexander, 39, for St. Louis in 1926.

Miscellaneous Multiple Choice

1. Freddie Lindstrom who was 18 years, 10 months and 13 days old when he played for the New York Giants against Washington in 1924.

2. Jack Quinn, 46 when he pitched for the Philadelphia Athletics in 1930.

3. Lou Boudreau, 24 years old when he played shortstop and managed the Cleveland Indians in 1942.

4. Detroit's Al Kaline, 20 in 1955.

5. Brooklyn's Pete Reiser, 22 in 1941.

6. Boston's Ted Williams, 40 in 1958.

7. Pittsburgh's Honus Wagner, 37 in 1911.

8. Kansas City's Bret Saberhagen, 21 in 1985.

9. New York Met Dwight Gooden, 20 in 1985.

10. Chicago's Early Wynn, 39 in 1959.

11. Philadelphia's Steve Carlton, 37 in 1982.

12. Detroit's Mickey Cochrane, 1934.

13. Cincinnati's Frank McCormick, 1940.

14. The Yankees' Bobby Richardson, 1960.

15. The Dodgers' Larry Sherry, 1959.

16. The Yankees' Thurman Munson, 1970.

17. The Yankees' Bobby Shantz won the award, 1957–1960.

18. New York's Ron Guidry, 1982–1986.

19. St. Louis' Bob Gibson, nine consecutive years, 1965–1973.

20. Cincinnati's Tom Browning, a 1–0 victory over the Dodgers on September 16, 1988.

21. Oakland's Catfish Hunter, a 4–0 victory over Minnesota on May 8, 1968.

22. Chicago's Charlie Robertson, a 2–0 win over Detroit on April 30, 1922.

23. Philadelphia's Jim Bunning, a 6–0 victory over the Mets on June 21, 1964.

24. An AL game by Boston's Cy Young, 3–0 over Philadelphia on May 5, 1904.

25. Babe Ruth, .847 in 1920.

26. George Sisler, 257 for the St. Louis Browns in 1920.

27. Chicago's Hack Wilson, 56 in 1930.

28. Pittsburgh's Kiki Cuyler, 26 in 1925.

29. Kansas City's Willie Wilson, 705 in 1980.

30. Detroit's George Kell, 56 in 1950.

31. Babe Ruth, 170 in 1923.

32. Bobby Bonds, 189 times in 1970.

33. Jose Morales, 25 for Montreal in 1976.

34. Buddy Rosar, Philadelphia Athletics, 1946.

35. Steve Garvey, with San Diego in 1984.

36. Chuck Klein, 44 for the Phillies in 1930.

37. Ted Williams, .344.

38. Pete Rose, 3,562.

39. Eddie Collins, 2,826 games.

40. Dave Winfield, 2,850 games through 1993.

41. Tris Speaker, 793 doubles. Rose hit 746.

42. Sam Crawford, 312 triples.

43. Manny Mota, 150.

44. Rickey Henderson, 1,095 of them through 1993.

45. Willie Stargell, 1,936 strikeouts.

46. Tris Speaker, 450 assists. Cobb had 392.

47. Mickey Mantle, 42.

48. Yogi Berra, 71.

49. Christy Mathewson.

50. Whitey Ford.

Trades

1. Roger Maris.

2. The pitcher was Vida Blue. The seven Giants were Gary Alexander, Gary Thomasson, Dave Heaverlo, Alan Wirth, John Henry Johnson, Phil Huffman and Mario Guerrero.

3. Bobby Murcer.

4. Mickey Rivers and Ed Figueroa.

5. Jose DeLeon.

6. The Yankees traded Lew Burdette (and $50,000) for Johnny Sain.

7. The Phillies acquired Steve Carlton for Rick Wise.

8. On June 15, 1983, the Mets got first baseman Keith Hernandez from the Cardinals for Neil Allen and Rick Ownbey. On December 10, 1984, they acquired catcher Gary Carter from Montreal for Hubie Brooks, Mike Fitzgerald, Herm Winningham and Floyd Youmans.

9. Sparky Lyle.

10. The Yankees traded Billy Martin, along with Woodie Held, Ralph Terry and Bob Martyn, for relief pitcher Ryne Duren, along with Jim Pisoni, Milt Graff and Harry Simpson.

11. On August 10, 1960, Detroit sent their manager Jimmy Dykes to Cleveland in exchange for Cleveland's manager, Joe Gordon. Even with this unusual managerial exchange, both teams finished under .500 for the year and out of the money in the American League.

12. Amos Rusie.

13. Charles Williams (and $50,000).

14. Pittsburgh sent Gene Michael (and Bob Bailey) to Los Angeles for Maury Wills.

15. Rick Monday.

16. Pitcher Milt Pappas, along with Jack Baldschun and Dick Simpson.

17. Bob Johnson and Amos Otis.

18. Nolan Ryan, along with Leroy Stanton, Don Rose and Francisco Estrada.

19. Ken Brett, Dock Ellis and Willie Randolph.

All-Star Games

1. Connie Mack of the Philadelphia Athletics managed the American League to a 4–2 victory over the National League led by John McGraw of the New York Giants.

2. Fred Lynn of the California Angels in the 1983 game, which the American League won, 13–3.

3. Pittsburgh's Arky Vaughan, 1941; Boston's Ted Williams, 1946; Cleveland's Al Rosen, 1954; San Francisco's Willie McCovey, 1969; Montreal's Gary Carter, 1981.

4. Nolan Ryan, 42 when he won the 1989 game for the AL, 5–3.

5. Dwight Gooden, 19 when he pitched in the 1984 game.

6. Babe Ruth, Lou Gehrig, Jimmie Foxx, Al Simmons and Joe Cronin.

7. Willie Mays, 6.

8. Stan Musial, Willie Mays and Hank Aaron.

9. Musial, 6.

10. No. That record goes to Ted Williams, with 12.

Home Runs

1. Reggie Jackson, 6th on the list with 563.

2. Three. Johnny Bench, 389 home runs, Carlton Fisk, 375, and Yogi Berra, 358.

3. Two. Duke Snider, 406 home runs, and Gil Hodges, 370.

4. Cecil Fielder, Detroit, 51 in 1990.

5. George Foster, Cincinnati, 52 in 1977.

6. Babe Ruth, 12.

7. Detroit's Hank Greenberg hit 39 of his 58 home runs at home in 1938.

8. Jimmy Foxx, 58 for the Philadelphia Athletics in 1932, and Hank Greenberg, 58 for the Detroit Tigers in 1938.

9. Two. Nick Etten led the AL with 22 home runs in 1944, and Graig Nettles did the same with 32 in 1976.

10. Rabbit Maranville, 672 at bats with the 1922 Pittsburgh Pirates.

11. Vern Stephens, with 24 in 1945.

12. Larry Doby, with 32 for Cleveland in 1952.

13. The 1961 Yankees, with Roger Maris, 61 home runs, and Mickey Mantle, 54.

14. One. Gus Zernial led the American League in home runs with 33 in 1951 when he played for both the White Sox and the Athletics.

15. One, Jim Tobin of the Boston Braves, on May 13, 1942.

16. Yes, Tony Cloninger for the Atlanta Braves on July 3, 1966.

17. The Pirates' Ralph Kiner and New York Giants' Johnny Mize tied for the National League lead in home runs with 51 in 1947, and again with 40 in 1948.

18. Dolph Camilli, with 34 in 1941.

19. Yes, Eddie Mathews with 47 in 1953 and again with 46 in 1959.

20. New York Yankee Don Mattingly, 6 in 1987.

21. Lou Gehrig, 23.

22. Stan Musial, 475 career home runs.

23. Wes Ferrell, 38 between 1927 and 1941.

24. St. Louis Cardinal Mark Whiten, September 7, 1993.

25. Lou Gehrig, Pat Seerey, Rocky Colavito, Chuck Klein, Gil Hodges, Joe Adcock, Willie Mays, Mike Schmidt and Bob Horner.

Batting Average Leaders

1. Rod Carew, Minnesota Twins, 1972 through 1975, and Wade Boggs, Boston Red Sox, 1985 through 1988.

2. Rogers Hornsby, St. Louis, six years, 1920 through 1925.

3. No. That record goes to Nap Lajoie of the Philadelphia Athletics, who led the AL with a .422 average in 1901.

4. George Brett, Kansas City, .390 in 1980.

5. Stan Musial, St. Louis, .376 in 1948.

6. One. Harry Walker led the National League with a .363 average in 1947 when he played for both St. Louis and Philadelphia.

7. One. Dale Alexander led the AL with a .367 average in 1932, playing for both Detroit and Boston.

8. Ty Cobb, 12.

9. Cleveland's Joe Jackson hit .408 in 1911 and was second to Ty Cobb's .420.

10. George Sternweiss, .309 in 1945, and Don Mattingly, .343 in 1984.

11. Cleveland outfielder Tris Speaker led the AL with a .386 average in 1916. Cobb was second at .371.

12. Philadelphia's Al Simmons, .381 in 1930 and .390 in 1931.

13. Detroit's Harry Heilmann led the AL in batting with averages of .394 in 1921, .403 in 1923, .393 in 1925 and .398 in 1927.

14. Norm Cash, .361 in 1961.

15. Al Kaline, .340 in 1955, and Harvey Kuenn, .353 in 1959.

16. George Kell, .343 in 1949.

17. Yes, Carl Furillo, .344 in 1953.

18. Tommy Davis, .346 in 1962 and .326 in 1963.

19. One, Richie Ashburn, but he won it twice—.338 in 1955 and .350 in 1958.

The Great Teams and Their Players

1. Cy Young (28–9), Bill Dinneen (21–13) and Long Tom Hughes (20–7).

2. Nap Lajoie of Cleveland, .355.

3. Pittsburgh.

4. Honus Wagner, with .355.

5. John McGraw.

6. Joe McGinnity (35–8) and Christy Mathewson (33–12).

7. Joe Tinker, Johnny Evers and Frank Chance.

8. Harry Steinfeldt.

9. Frank Chance.

10. Ty Cobb, with .350 in 1907 and .324 in 1908.

11. Sam Crawford.

12. Connie Mack, Philadelphia Athletics.

13. Jack Coombs.

14. Eddie Collins, .322 in 1910 and .365 in 1911.

15. Smoky Joe Wood.

16. No. Brooklyn's Jake Daubert led the NL with a .329 average.

17. Harry Hooper.

18. No, the second. Boston's Patsy Dougherty hit two in the second game of the first World Series in 1903.

19. Babe Ruth.

20. Benny Kauff.

21. Red Faber, Chicago White Sox. Chicago beat the Giants in six games.

22. White Sox outfielder Shoeless Joe Jackson in a losing effort in the last game.

23. Cleveland, 5–2 over Brooklyn. (For a few years around this time the Series went to the first team to win five games instead of the traditional four.)

24. Elmer Smith.

25. Jim Bagby.

26. Billy Wambsganss.

27. Stan Covaleski.

28. Rogers Hornsby, .370, for the NL St. Louis Cardinals; George Sisler, .407, for the AL Browns.

29. Bob Meusel for the Yankees, Emil (Irish) Meusel for the Giants.

30. Casey Stengel.

31. Pittsburgh, in four games.

32. Shortstop Mark Koenig, .500 (9 for 18).

33. Miller Huggins.

34. Waite Hoyt, 22–7.

35. Howard Ehmke.

36. Pepper Martin.

37. Charlie Root.

38. Yes.

39. No, but Yankee second baseman Tony Lazzeri did.

40. Mel Ott.

41. One, Carl Hubbell, 23–12.

42. Bill Terry.

43. St. Louis Cardinals Dizzy and Paul Dean.

44. The Gashouse Gang.

45. Frankie Frisch.

46. Detroit, in seven games.

47. Goose Goslin, as the Tigers beat the Cubs in six.

48. Mickey Cochrane.

49. Joe DiMaggio.

50. Joe McCarthy.

51. Lefty Gomez, five.

52. The St. Louis Cardinals, in five games.

53. St. Louis' third baseman, Whitey Kurowski.

54. Chicago Cub Hank Borowy, who beat Detroit on October 3, 1945 in the first game of the 1945 World Series.

55. No, the Tigers won in 7.

56. Five.

57. Only once, 103 wins in 1954.

58. Despite the 103 wins, they finished second, eight games behind Cleveland.

59. Allie Reynolds, six.

60. Johnny Mize, in the 3rd, 4th and 5th games in 1952.

61. Billy Martin.

62. Gil McDougald, in 1951.

63. Phil Rizzuto.

64. Early Wynn, 23; Bob Lemon, 23; Mike Garcia, 19; Art Houtteman, 15; Bob Feller, 13.

65. They lost to the Giants in four straight games.

66. Johnny Podres.

67. Sandy Amoros.

68. Yogi Berra.

69. Duke Snider.

70. Johnny Kucks.

71. Don Larsen.

72. Sal Maglie.

73. Lew Burdette.

74. Dodger righthander Don Drysdale, in Game 3 of the 1959 Series between Los Angeles and the Chicago White Sox.

75. Walter Alston, Dodgers, and Al Lopez, White Sox.

76. No. Yankee second baseman Bobby Richardson drove in a record 12 in the same Series.

77. Bill Mazeroski.

78. Ralph Terry.

79. Danny Murtaugh.

80. Roger Maris, 61; Mickey Mantle, 54; Bill Skowron, 28; Yogi Berra, 22; Elston Howard, 21; Johnny Blanchard, 21.

81. Yes, in five games against Cincinnati.

82. All of them except Mantle, who was limited by injuries to six times at bat.

83. Joe Pepitone.

84. Sandy Koufax, Don Drysdale, Johnny Podres and Ron Perranoski.

85. Jim Bouton.

86. Johnny Keane.

87. Yogi Berra.

88. Frank Robinson.

89. Hank Bauer.

90. St. Louis' Bob Gibson in 1967 as the Cardinals beat Boston in seven; Detroit's Mickey Lolich in 1968 as the Tigers defeated the Cardinals, also in seven.

91. Yes.

92. Gil Hodges.

93. One, Tom Seaver, 25–7.

94. Donn Clendenon and Al Weis.

95. Charles O. Finley.

96. Dick Williams in 1972 and 1973; Alvin Dark in 1974.

97. Catcher–first baseman Gene Tenace, 4 (all of them in 1972).

98. Joe Morgan.

99. Thirty-five years, since 1940.

100. Luis Tiant.

101. Sparky Anderson.

102. Cincinnati swept New York in four games, but Yankee catcher Thurman Munson batted .529 (9 for 17), almost as good as Johnny Bench's .533 (8 for 15).

103. Tommy Lasorda, Dodgers; Billy Martin, 1977 Yankees; Bob Lemon, 1978 Yankees.

104. Two. New York's Reggie Jackson hit his record-tying five in 1977; Dodger Davey Lopes hit three in 1978.

105. Mike Torrez.

106. Graig Nettles.

107. The Philadelphia Phillies.

108. Tug McGraw.

109. Pedro Guerrero.

110. Joaquin Andujar.

111. Bret Saberhagen.

112. Dick Howser.

113. Bill Buckner.

114. Catcher Gary Carter, 9.

115. Kirk Gibson.

116. Orel Hershiser.

117. Jack Morris.

118. Dave Winfield.

119. Jimmy Key.

120. Joe Carter.

121. Paul Molitor, Toronto's designated hitter.

Brothers

1. Hank Aaron hit 755 and his brother Tommie hit 13 for a combined 768.

2. No. The three DiMaggio brothers hold that honor with a combined 2,739 RBIs (Joe had 1,537, Dom had 618 and Vince had 584).

3. Phil and Joe Niekro won 539 games, and Gaylord and Jim Perry won 529 games.

4. Paul and Lloyd Waner got 5,611 hits and Felipe, Matty and Jesus Alou got 5,094.

5. Tony Conigliaro (36) and his brother Billy (18) combined for 54 home runs for the Red Sox in 1970.

6. Paul (19) and Dizzy (30) Dean won 49 games for the 1934 Cardinals.

7. Harry and Stan Coveleski. Harry won 22 for the 1914 Tigers, and Stan won 22 for the 1918 Cleveland Indians.

8. Rick and Paul Reuschel of the Chicago Cubs combined to beat the Los Angeles Dodgers by the score of 7–0 on August 21, 1975.

A Pitching Quiz

1. Hoyt Wilhelm, 1,070 games, and Kent Tekulve, 1,050.

2. Warren Spahn, 363.

3. Cy Young, 511; Walter Johnson, 416; Christy Mathewson, 373; Grover Cleveland Alexander, 373.

4. Nolan Ryan, 10.

5. Phil Niekro, 5,403⅔; Nolan Ryan, 5,387; Gaylord Perry, 5,352; Don Sutton, 5,281⅔; Warren Spahn, 5,246; Steve Carlton, 5,216⅓.

6. Walter Johnson, 110.

7. Nolan Ryan, 2,795.

8. Hoyt Wilhelm, 124; Lindy McDaniel, 119; Goose Gossage, 108 through 1992; Rollie Fingers, 107.

9. Nolan Ryan, 383 for the California Angels in 1973.

10. Mike Marshall, 106 for the Dodgers in 1974.

11. Bob Gibson, 1.12 for St. Louis in 1968.

12. Grover Cleveland Alexander, 16 for the Philadelphia Phillies in 1916.

13. Bob Gibson, 13 for St. Louis in 1968.

14. Walter Johnson, 206.

15. Lefty Grove, 9.

16. Sandy Koufax, in the five seasons 1962–1966.

17. Bill Fischer, Kansas City Athletics, 84⅓ innings in 1962.

18. Denny McLain, 31 for Detroit in 1968.

19. Lefty Grove, 31 for Philadelphia in 1931.

20. Dizzy Dean, 30 for St. Louis in 1934.

21. 41 by Jack Chesbro for New York in the AL in 1904.

22. Warren Spahn, 8 times.

23. Cy Young, 16 times.

24. Steve Carlton, 27 for Philadelphia in 1972.

25. No.

26. Ron Guidry, 25 in 1978.

27. Sandy Koufax, 27 in 1966.

28. Cy Young, Jim Bunning, Gaylord Perry, Ferguson Jenkins, Nolan Ryan.

29. Wilbur Wood for the Chicago White Sox against the Yankees on July 20, 1973.

30. He lost both games.

31. Ed Reulbach for the Cubs against Brooklyn on September 26, 1908. The scores were 5–0 and 3–0.

32. Bo Belinsky for the (then) Los Angeles Angels against Baltimore on May 5, 1962.

33. Bob Feller for Cleveland against Chicago in 1940.

34. Nolan Ryan, 7.

35. San Francisco Giant Jim Barr: 41 in a row over two games in 1972.

36. Bernie Carbo.

37. Carl Hubbell, 24 for the New York Giants, 1936–1937.

38. Gaylord Perry, with Cleveland in the AL in 1972 and San Diego in the NL, 1978.

39. Tony Cloninger, for Atlanta on July 3, 1966.

40. None.

41. Leon Cadore of Brooklyn and Joe Oeschger of the Boston Braves pitched a record 26 innings against each other on May 1, 1920. The game ended in a 1–1 tie.

42. Whitey Ford, .690: 236 wins, 106 losses.

43. Tom Seaver, 10, on April 22, 1970 against San Diego.

44. Tom Seaver, 9: 1968–1976.

Most Valuable Player/Cy Young Award Winners

1. Jimmy Foxx, Philadelphia, 1932–1933; Hal Newhouser, Detroit, 1944–1945; Yogi Berra, New York, 1954–1955; Mickey Mantle, New York, 1956–1957; Roger Maris, New York, 1960–1961.

2. Five. Ernie Banks, Chicago, 1958–1959; Joe Morgan, Cincinnati, 1975–1976; Mike Schmidt, Philadelphia, 1980–1981; Dale Murphy, Atlanta, 1982–1983; Barry Bonds, San Francisco, 1992–1993.

3. The award was inaugurated in 1931 by Lefty Grove, Philadelphia Athletics, in the AL, and Frankie Frisch, St. Louis Cardinals, in the NL.

4. Dennis Eckersley, Oakland, 1992, in the AL; Bob Gibson, St. Louis, 1968, in the NL.

5. Don Newcombe, Brooklyn.

6. Bobby Shantz, Philadelphia Athletics, 1952; Denny McLain, Detroit Tigers, 1968; Vida Blue, Oakland Athletics, 1971.

7. One, Fred Lynn, Boston Red Sox, 1975.

8. Frank Robinson, Cincinnati (NL), 1961, and Baltimore (AL), 1966.

9. Pittsburgh Pirate Willie Stargell, 39 in 1979.

10. Cincinnati's Johnny Bench, 22 in 1970.

11. Jim Konstanty, Phillies, 1950; Don Newcombe, Dodgers, 1956; Sandy Koufax, Dodgers, 1963; Bob Gibson, Cardinals, 1968.

12. Roger Maris, Mickey Mantle, Elston Howard, New York Yankees, 1961–1963.

13. No. Joe DiMaggio, Joe Gordon, and Spud Chandler won consecutive MVPs for the Yankees in 1941–1943.

14. Mort Cooper, Stan Musial and Marty Marion won consecutive MVPs for the Cardinals in 1942–1944.

15. No. Ernie Lombardi, Bucky Walters and Frank McCormick won consecutive MVPs for the Cincinnati Reds in 1938–1940.

16. The Yankees' Bob Turley, 1958.

17. Steve Carlton, Philadelphia Phillies, 1972, 1977, 1980 and 1982.

18. Fernando Valenzuela, Dodgers, 1981.

Managers

1. In the AL, Connie Mack, 50 years with the Philadelphia Athletics, 1901–1950. In the NL, John McGraw managed the New York Giants for 31 seasons, 1902–1932.

2. McGraw does indeed hold the NL record with 10 pennants, but Casey Stengel holds the AL mark, also 10, with the Yankees.

3. Casey Stengel and Joe McCarthy, both with the Yankees.

4. Bill McKechnie, Pittsburgh, 1925; St. Louis, 1928; Cincinnati, 1939, 1940. Dick Williams, Boston, 1967; Oakland, 1972, 1973; San Diego, 1984.

5. Gene Mauch, 26 seasons with several teams between 1960 and 1987.

6. Joe McCarthy, .615 over 24 seasons, 2,125 wins and 1,333 losses.

7. Lou Boudreau, Cleveland, 1948.

8. Once, Clark Griffith, Chicago, 1901.

Nicknames

1. Max Carey.

2. George Kelly.

3. Johnny Mize.

4. Carlton Fisk.

5. Keith Hernandez.

6. Luke Appling.

7. Willie Mays.

8. Miller Huggins.

9. Frank Chance.

10. Herry Heilmann.

11. Phil Rizzuto.

12. Roger Bresnahan.

13. Bill Madlock.

14. Greg Luzinski.

15. Ron Cey.

16. Ralph Garr.

17. Travis Jackson.

18. Joe Medwick.

19. John McGraw.

20. Dave Bancroft.

21. Connie Mack.

22. Dave Parker.

23. Charlie Gehringer.

24. Reggie Jackson.

25. Willie McCovey.

26. Orlando Cepeda.

27. Willie Keeler.

28. Tommy Henrich.

29. Don Mueller.

30. Billy Hamilton.

31. Jim Bottomley.

32. Frankie Frisch.

33. Rogers Hornsby.

34. Walter James Vincent Maranville.

35. Pee Wee Reese.

36. Earle Combs.

37. Tony Lazzeri.

38. Pepper Martin.

39. Lou Gehrig.

40. Charles Leo Hartnett.

41. Marty Marion.

42. Frank Howard.

43. Leo Durocher.

44. Carl Furillo.

45. Ken Harrelson.

46. Jimmie Foxx.

47. Rusty Staub.

48. Frank Edwin McGraw.

49. Jim Grant.

50. Lloyd (Little Poison) Waner and Paul (Big Poison) Waner.

51. Elwin Charles Roe.

52. Steve Carlton.

53. Sal Maglie.

54. Riggs Stephenson.

55. Bill Skowron.

56. Joseph Jerome McGinnity.

57. Vernon Louis "Lefty" Gomez.

58. Honus Wagner.

59. Jim Hunter.

60. Phil Niekro.

61. Whitey Ford.

62. Luis Arroyo.

63. Juan Marichal.

64. Lon Warneke.

65. George Selkirk.

66. Burleigh Grimes.

67. Ed Lopat.

68. Vic Raschi.

69. Eddie Stankey.

70. Ted Williams.

71. Fred Marberry.

72. Tom Henke.

73. Mordecai Peter Centennial Brown.

74. Ozzie Smith.

75. Bob Feller.

76. Richard Michael Gossage.

77. Hal Newhouser.

78. Amos Rusie.

79. James Francis "Pud" Galvin.

80. Early Wynn.

81. Ron Guidry.

82. Sam McDowell.

83. Dixie Walker.

84. Tris Speaker.

85. Eddie Yost.

86. Jay Hanna Dean.

87. Walter Johnson.

88. Mike Garcia.

89. Enos Slaughter.

90. Zoilo Versalles.

91. Robert Moses "Lefty" Grove.

92. Christy Mathewson.

93. Clarence Arthur Vance.

94. Adolfo Luque.

95. Casey Stengel.

96. Leslie Ambrose Bush.

97. Johnny Murphy.

98. Lynwood Thomas Rowe.

99. Carl Hubbell.

100. Harvey Haddix.

101. Harry Walker.

102. Harold Joseph Traynor.

103. Carl Erskine.

104. Eldon Auker.

105. Leon Wagner.

106. Walt Williams.

107. Dick Stuart.